PIANO/VOCAL SELECTIONS

MW00785583

Disney Theatrical Productions
under the direction of
Thomas Schumacher

Presents

Music by	*Lyrics by*	*Book by*
ALAN MENKEN	**JACK FELDMAN**	**HARVEY FIERSTEIN**

Based on the Disney film written by BOB TZUDIKER and NONI WHITE

Starring

JEREMY JORDAN

JOHN DOSSETT   KARA LINDSAY   CAPATHIA JENKINS   BEN FANKHAUSER

ANDREW KEENAN-BOLGER   LEWIS GROSSO   MATTHEW J. SCHECHTER

AARON J. ALBANO   MARK ALDRICH   TOMMY BRACCO   JOHN E. BRADY   RYAN BRESLIN
KEVIN CAROLAN   CAITLYN CAUGHELL   KYLE COFFMAN   MIKE FAIST   MICHAEL FATICA
JULIE FOLDESI   GARETT HAWE   THAYNE JASPERSON   EVAN KASPRZAK   JESS LePROTTO
STUART MARLAND   ANDY RICHARDSON   JACK SCOTT   RYAN STEELE   BRENDON STIMSON
NICK SULLIVAN   EPHRAIM SYKES   LAURIE VELDHEER   ALEX WONG   STUART ZAGNIT

Scenic Design	*Costume Design*	*Lighting Design*	*Sound Design*
TOBIN OST	**JESS GOLDSTEIN**	**JEFF CROITER**	**KEN TRAVIS**

Projection Design	*Hair & Wig Design*	*Fight Direction*	*Casting*
SVEN ORTEL	**CHARLES G. LAPOINTE**	**J. ALLEN SUDDETH**	**TELSEY + COMPANY** **JUSTIN HUFF, CSA**

Associate Producer	*Technical Supervision*	*Production Manager*	*Production Stage Manager*
ANNE QUART	**NEIL MAZZELLA &** **GEOFFREY QUART**	**EDUARDO CASTRO**	**THOMAS J. GATES**

Music Director/ *Dance Music Arrangements*	*Music Coordinator*	*Associate Director*	*Associate Choreographer*
MARK HUMMEL	**JOHN MILLER**	**RICHARD J. HINDS**	**LOU CASTRO**

Orchestrations by
DANNY TROOB

Music Supervision
Incidental Music & Vocal Arrangements by
MICHAEL KOSARIN

Choreographed by
CHRISTOPHER GATTELLI

Directed by
JEFF CALHOUN

World Premiere, Paper Mill Playhouse, in Millburn, New Jersey, on September 25, 2011.
Mark S. Hoebee, Producing Artistic Director, Todd Schmidt, Managing Director

©Disney

ISBN 978-1-4584-7722-4

Photography by Deen van Meer

WONDERLAND MUSIC COMPANY, INC.

DISTRIBUTED BY

7777 W. BLUEMOUND RD. P.O. BOX 13819 MILWAUKEE, WI 53213

In Australia Contact:
Hal Leonard Australia Pty. Ltd.
4 Lentara Court
Cheltenham, Victoria, 3192 Australia
Email: ausadmin@halleonard.com.au

Visit Hal Leonard Online at
www.halleonard.com

TROLLEY STRIKE ENTERS THIRD WEEK

Starving Workers Battle Profiteering Trolley Companies; Innocent Riding Public Suffers

DAVID VS. GOLIATH AT THE BRINK OF A NEW CENTURY

By K. Plumber

With all eyes fixed on the trolley strike, there's another battle brewing in the city. A modern-day David is poised to take on the rich and powerful Goliath. With the swagger of one twice his age, armed with nothing more than a few nuggets of truth, Jack Kelly stands ready to face the behemoth Pulitzer. In the words of union leader Jack Kelly, "We will work with you. We will even work for you. But we will be paid and treated as valuable members of your organizations." Then he addressed the boys whom Pulitzer recruited as scabs: "For the sake of all the kids in every sweatshop, factory, and slaughter house in New York I beg you… join us."

Kyle Coffman

Headlines Don't Sell Papes Newsies Sell Papes

Ain't it a fine life, carrying the banner through it all! A mighty fine life, carrying the banner tough and tall. When that bell rings, we goes where we wishes. We's as free as fishes. Sure beats washin' dishes. What a fine life, carrying the banner home free all!

Jeremy Jordan, John Dossett

MOVEMENT APPEARS TO BE GROWING

The New Musical 'Newsies' Features Music by Alan Menken, Lyrics by Jack Feldman, and Book by Harvey Fierstein

They Dreamed of a Fair Shake and a Few Extra Pennies

JACK KELLY

An Unlikely Star Is Born
By K. Plumber

Picture a handsome, heroically charismatic, plain spoken, know-nothing skirt-chasing, cocky little flirt – complete egomaniac.

The fact is he's also the face of the strike. What a face! Face the fact: that's a face that could save us all from sinking in the ocean. Give those kids and me the brand new century and watch what happens! It's David and Goliath, do or die, the fight is on and I can't watch what happens. But all I know is nothing happens if you just give in. It can't be any worse than how it's been. And it just so happens that we just might win. So whatever happens, let's begin.

Andrew Keenan-Bolger, Jeremy Jordan

YOUNG MAN SETS SIGHTS WEST

Keep Your Small Life in the Big City – Give Me a Big Life in a Small Town

Jeremy Jordan

DOWNTOWN HISTORY MAKES UPTOWN DREAMS COME TRUE

By B. Tzudiker & N. White

In the summer of 1899, a bunch of tough kids selling newspapers on the streets of New York City dared to dream that children could stand up to two of the most powerful men in America. The newsies were briefly the kings of New York, effectively shutting down the papers owned by Joseph Pulitzer and William Randolph Hearst. Rival papers made heroes of the newsies, capturing their colorful slang – or making it up for a better quote. They paraded down Wall Street to showers of coins and drew politicians and performers to their rallies. Then the other publishers realized that these children controlled their distribution as well, and they could be next. So they colluded to suppress news of the strike, hoping that "If it's not in the papers, it never happened." Still, the kids pressed on, their strike spreading up and down the East Coast, until they won the respect and concessions they sought.

Ninety years later, this quintessential David and Goliath story gave us the courage to walk onto the Disney studio lot as first-time writers to pitch the film *Newsies*. Could these children, many of them homeless, have dreamed that almost a century later a movie and now a Broadway musical would celebrate their victory? For all we know, grandchildren of those newsies, now likely grandparents themselves, are applauding the show at the Nederlander Theatre, unaware of their personal connection to the history that took place on these very streets.

A FINE LIFE, CARRYING THE BANNER

Newsies on a Mission! Kill the Competition! Sell the Next Edition!

MEDDA LARKIN: A SENSATION!

Miss Medda Larkin, now a staple on the Bowery, is proving to be the greatest performer since Ada Overton Walker. She sings with a unique wit and sincerity. My guess is that she will be talk of the town soon enough. A highlight of the evening proves to be one of her new songs "That's Rich," with spry lyric and a whimsical melody all beautifully staged in front of a new pastoral backdrop. The Bowery Beauties, however, leave much to be desired. Their performance is quite flat and barely audible. Perhaps it is intentional that Miss Larkin far outshines the other talent on stage.

Now Is the Time to Seize the Day. Stare Down the Odds and Seize the Da Minute by Minute, That's How You Win It. We Will Find a Way.

Union president Jack Kelly addressed the newsies: "Pulitzer and Hearst, they think we're nothin'. Are we nothin'?" The newsies answered a resounding, "NO!" Again Kelly spoke: "Pulitzer and Hearst, they think they got us. Do they got us?" And again the response was: "NO!" followed by, "Even though we ain't got hats or badges, we're a union ju by saying so. Courage when we face our fear. T those in power, safe in the tower, we will not obey. B hold the brave battalion th stands side by side. Too fe in number and too proud hide. Then say to the othe who did not follow throug "You're still our brothers, a we will fight for you."

Mark Aldrich, Jeremy Jordan, Capathia Jenkins, Ben Fankhauser, Matthew J. Schechter

THE CHILDREN'S CRUSADE

Ten Thousand Kids in the Square, Ten Tousand Fists in the Air

THE NEWSIES' STRIKE ENDED TODAY WITH A HISTORIC COMPROMISE BETWEEN THE BEHEMOTH PULITZER AND THE RAG-TAG GANG OF RAGAMUFFINS.

ew York City came to a ndstill as children from all dustries dropped their la- rs and stormed Park Row. ew York is closed for busi- ss... paralyzed," said union ganizer, Jack Kelly. "You n't get a paper or a shoe ine. You can't send a mes- ge or ride an elevator or ss the Brooklyn Bridge."

Pulitzer was left with no choice but to negotiate with his independent distribution merchants. The publishers decreased the price hike only by half, but agreed to buy back any unsold papers. This shift in business model will have significant repercus- sions in the coming century.

"For the sake of all the kids in every sweatshop, factory, and slaughter house in New York I beg you... join us." – Jack Kelly

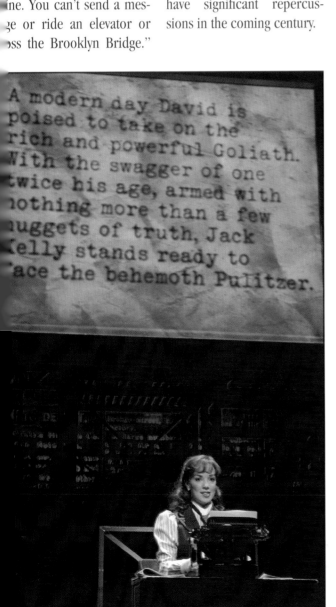

A modern day David is poised to take on the rich and powerful Goliath. With the swagger of one twice his age, armed with nothing more than a few nuggets of truth, Jack Kelly stands ready to face the behemoth Pulitzer.

Kara Lindsay

NEWSIES TRIUMPH

The Refuge Closes

Governor Theodore Roosevelt was on hand as The Refuge was shut down and the news- ies' strike ended in triumph. He addressed the mottled crowd, which also included messen- gers, telegraph boys, and fac- tory workers. "Each generation must, at the height of its power, step aside and invite the young to share the day. You have now laid claim to our world."

Matthew J. Schecter, Andrew Keenan-Bolger, Jess Leprotto, Mike Faist

CONTENTS

PROLOGUE (SANTA FE)

Music by ALAN MENKEN
Lyrics by JACK FELDMAN

Pastorale, freely

JACK: They say folks is dy-in' to get here. Me, I'm

dy-in' to get a-way to a lit-tle town out

West that's spank-in' new. And while

CARRYING THE BANNER

Music by ALAN MENKEN
Lyrics by JACK FELDMAN

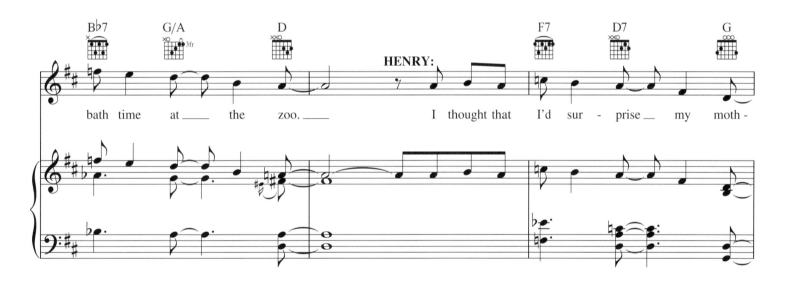

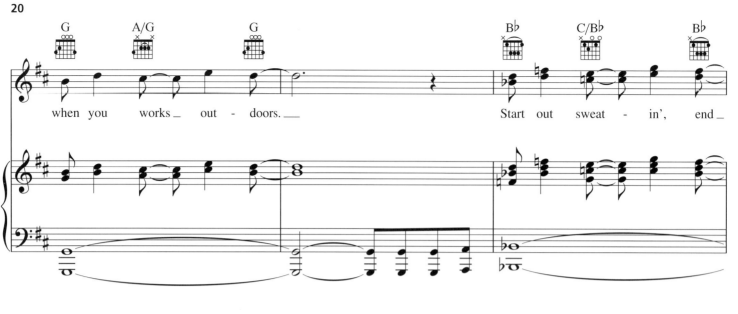

when you works _ out - doors. _ Start out sweat - in', end _

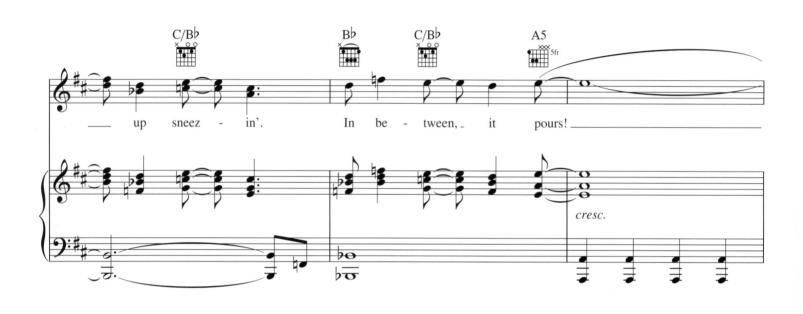

_ up sneez - in'. In be - tween, _ it pours! _

GROUP 1:
Still, it's a fine life, _ car - ry - ing the ban - ner with me

GROUP 2:
Still, it's a

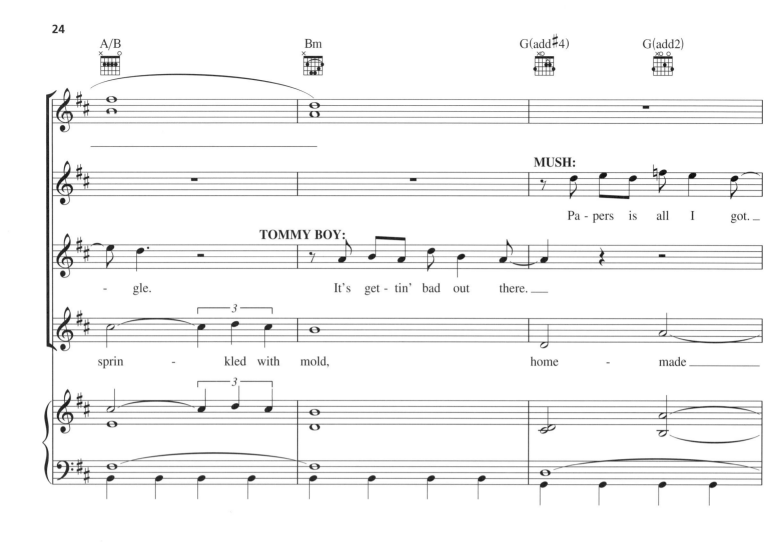

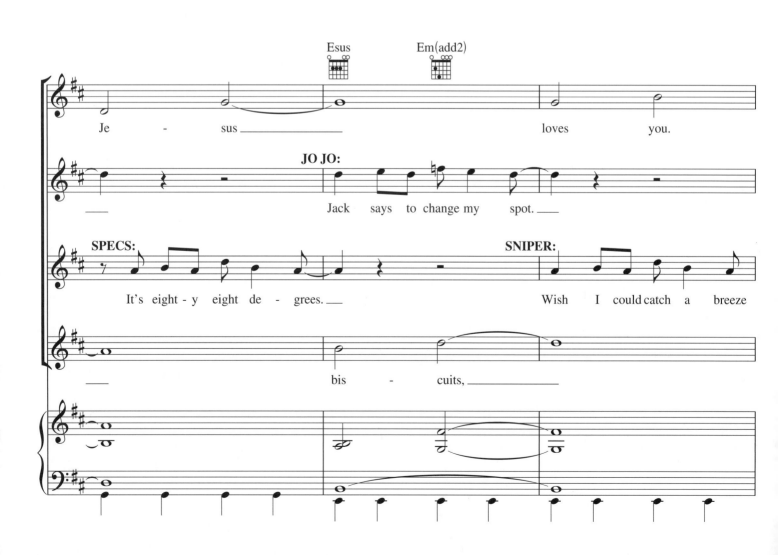

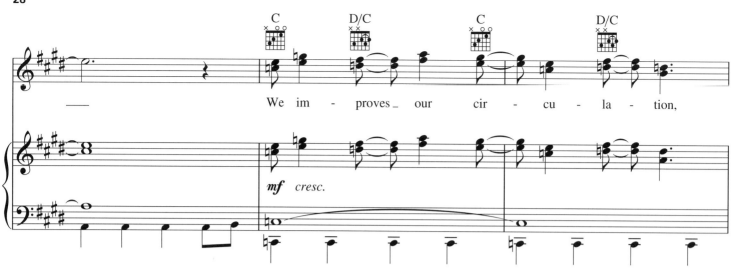

We im - proves_ our cir - cu - la - tion,

walk - in' till ___ we fall! ___

GROUP 1:

But we'll be

GROUP 2:

Got a

out there, _ car - ry - ing the ban - ner man to man.

feel - ing 'bout a head-line. I ___ smells me a head-line. Papes ___ are gon - na sell like we was

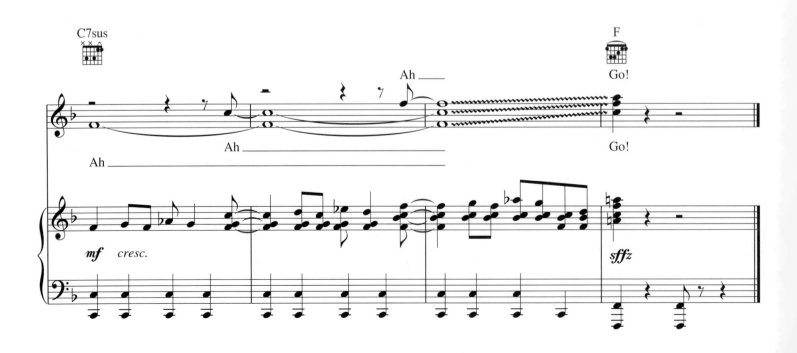

THE BOTTOM LINE

Music by ALAN MENKEN
Lyrics by JACK FELDMAN

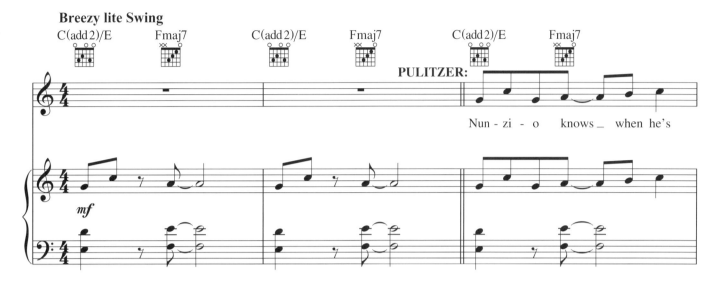

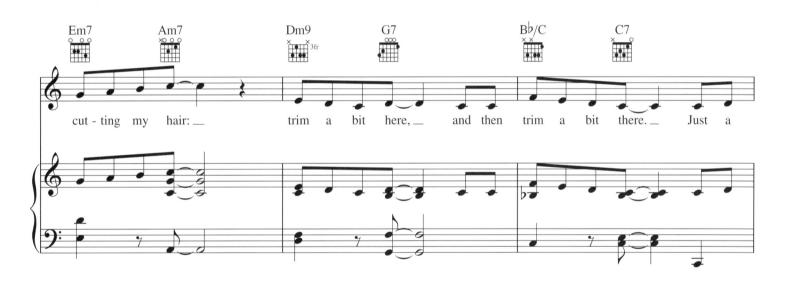

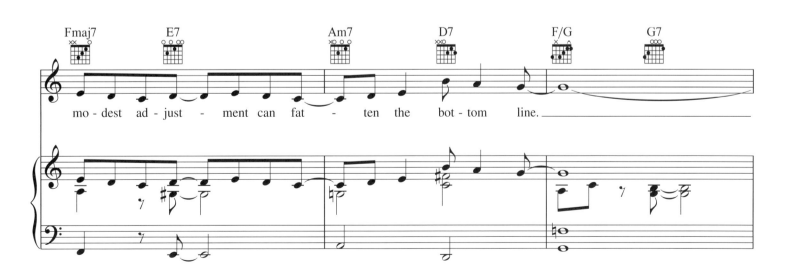

THAT'S RICH

Music by ALAN MENKEN
Lyrics by JACK FELDMAN

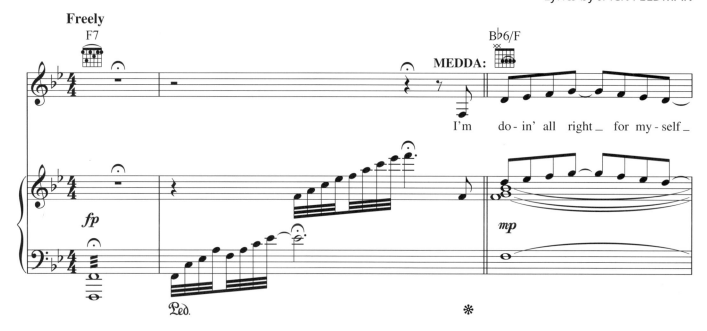

I'm do-in' all right_ for my-self_

__ folks. I'm health-y, I'm wealth-y, I'm wise.__ My in-

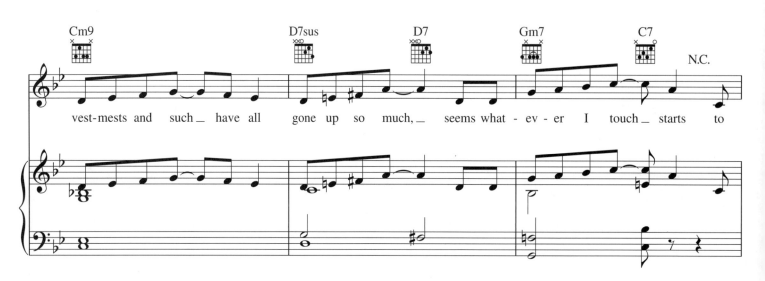

vest-mests and such_ have all gone up so much,_ seems what-ev-er I touch_ starts to

I NEVER PLANNED ON YOU/
DON'T COME A-KNOCKING

Music by ALAN MENKEN
Lyrics by JACK FELDMAN

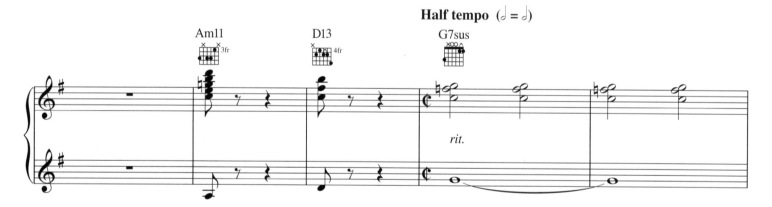

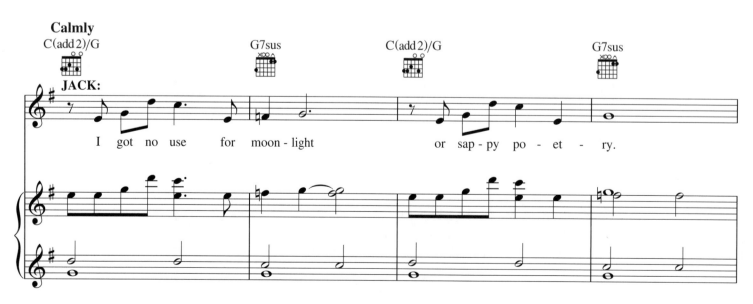

I got no use for moon-light or sap-py po-et-ry.

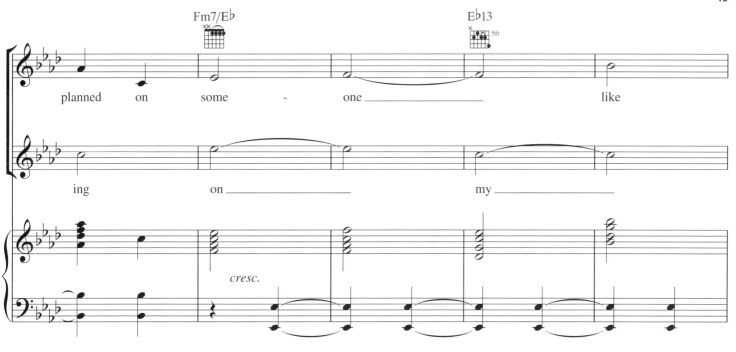

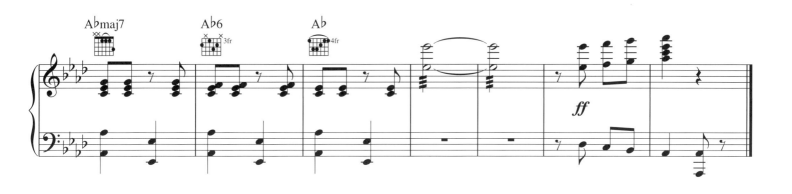

THE WORLD WILL KNOW

Music by ALAN MENKEN
Lyrics by JACK FELDMAN

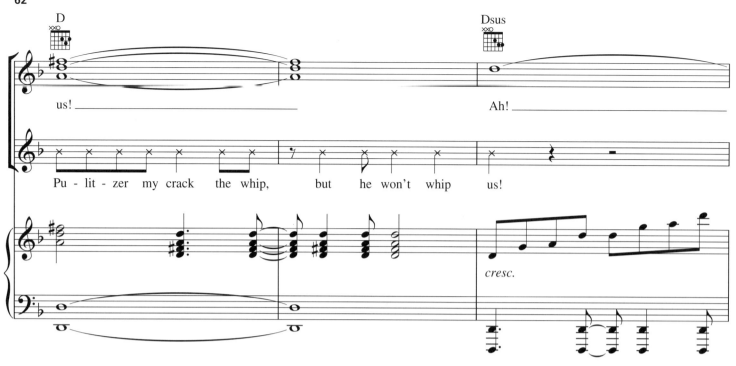

us! _____ Ah! _____

Pu - lit - zer my crack the whip, but he won't whip us!

cresc.

___ So the *World* says "No!" Well, the kids do too!

ff

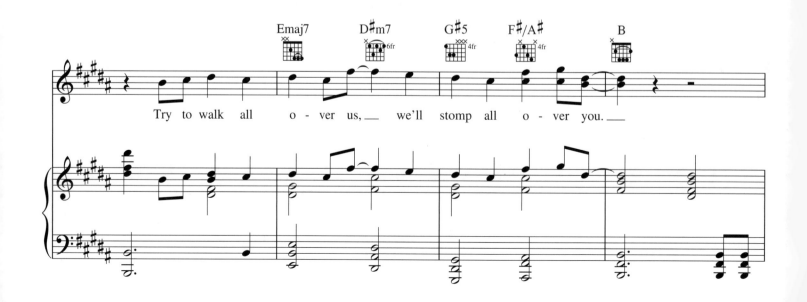

Try to walk all o - ver us, ___ we'll stomp all o - ver you. ___

63

WATCH WHAT HAPPENS

Music by ALAN MENKEN
Lyrics by JACK FELDMAN

Solidly, with drive

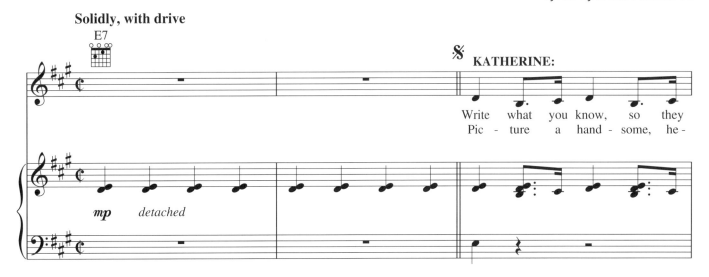

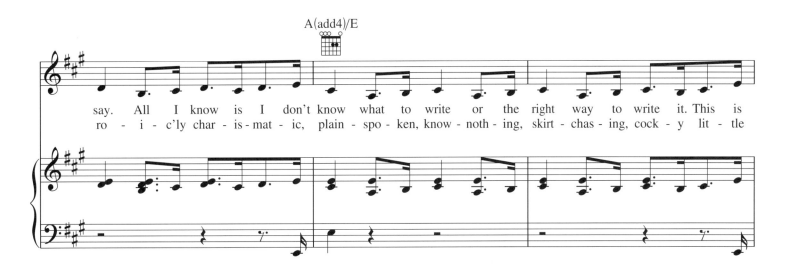

SEIZE THE DAY

Music by ALAN MENKEN
Lyrics by JACK FELDMAN

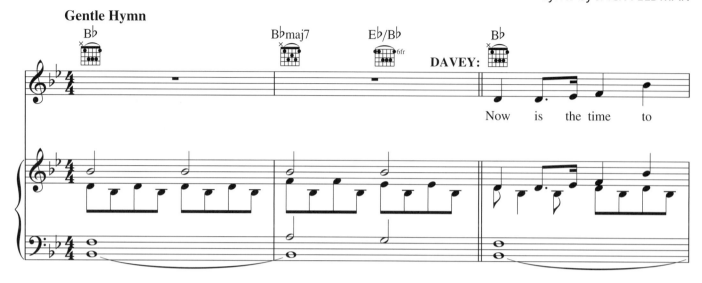

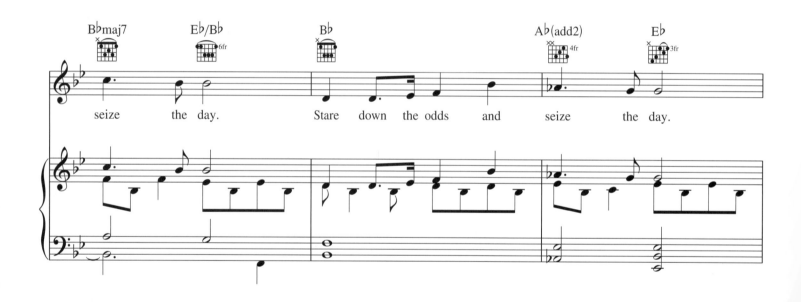

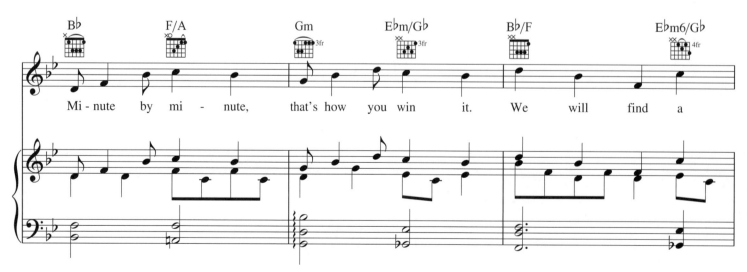

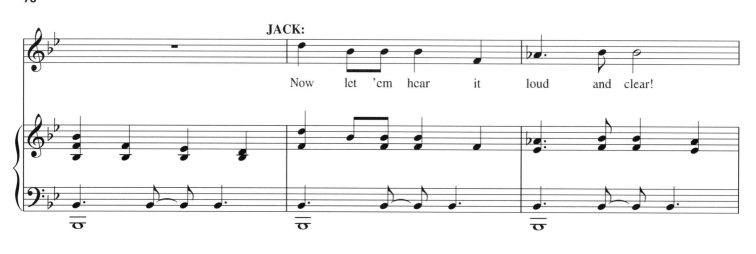

JACK:

Now let 'em hear it loud and clear!

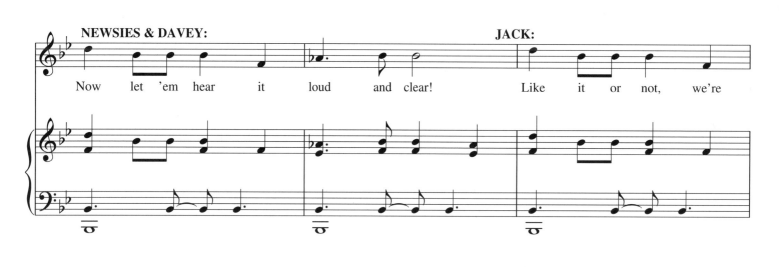

NEWSIES & DAVEY:

Now let 'em hear it loud and clear!

JACK:

Like it or not, we're

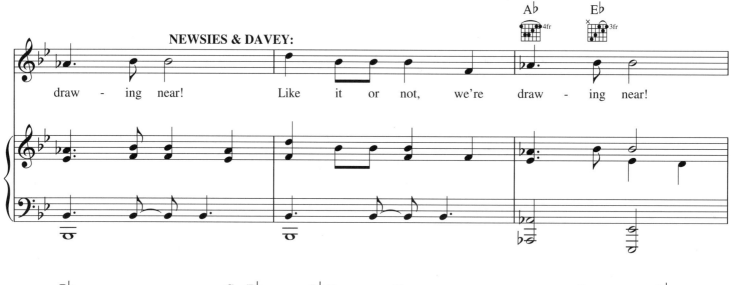

NEWSIES & DAVEY:

draw - ing near! Like it or not, we're draw - ing near!

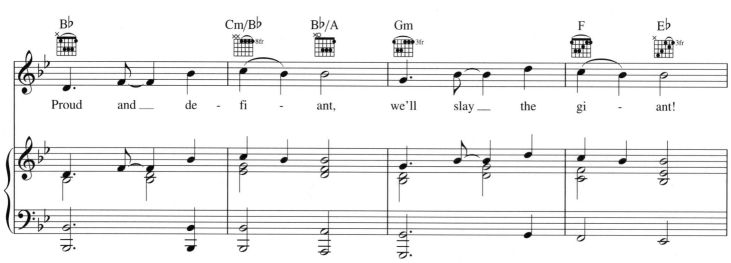

Proud and __ de - fi - ant, we'll slay __ the gi - ant!

SANTA FE

Music by ALAN MENKEN
Lyrics by JACK FELDMAN

KING OF NEW YORK

Music by ALAN MENKEN
Lyrics by JACK FELDMAN

there I be! Ain't ___ I pret - ty? It's ___ my ci - ty. I'm ___

___ the king ___ of New York!

JO JO: A so - lid gold watch with a chain to twirl ___ it. My

ver - y own bed and a in - door ter - let. A **MUSH:** bar - ber - shop hair - cut that

96

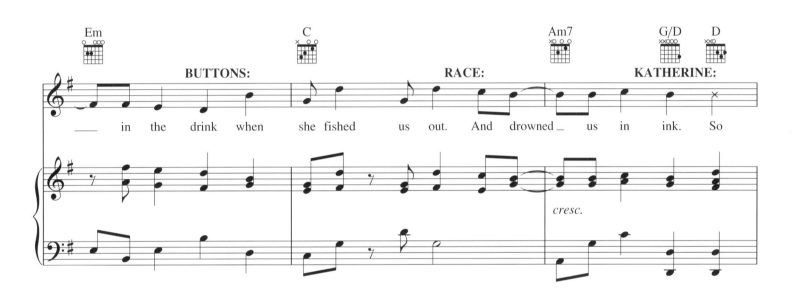

98

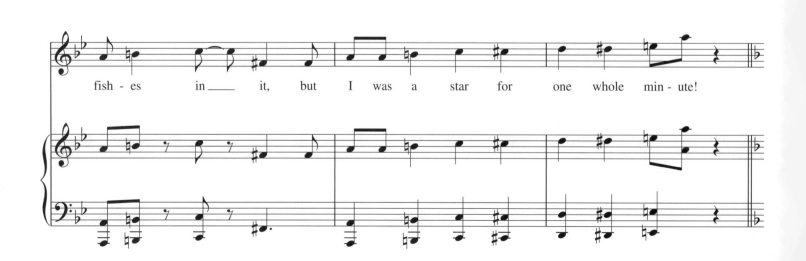

BROOKLYN'S HERE

Music by ALAN MENKEN
Lyrics by JACK FELDMAN

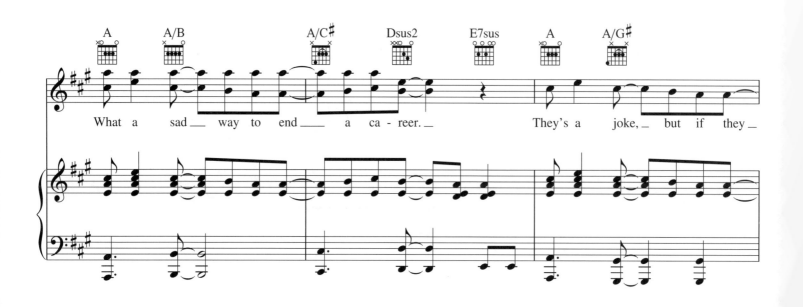

SOMETHING TO BELIEVE IN

Music by ALAN MENKEN
Lyrics by JACK FELDMAN

ONCE AND FOR ALL

Music by ALAN MENKEN
Lyrics by JACK FELDMAN

120

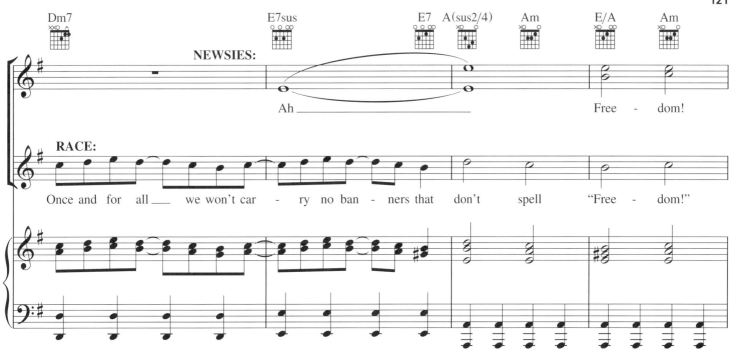

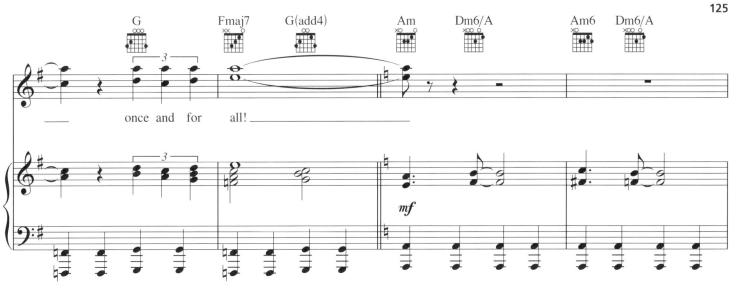

once and for all! _____

NEWSIES (Group 1):

Once and for

NEWSIES (Group 2):

Once and for all. _____

cresc. poco a poco

all. _____

Once and for

Once and for all. _____

Half-time feel, Hard Rock backbeat

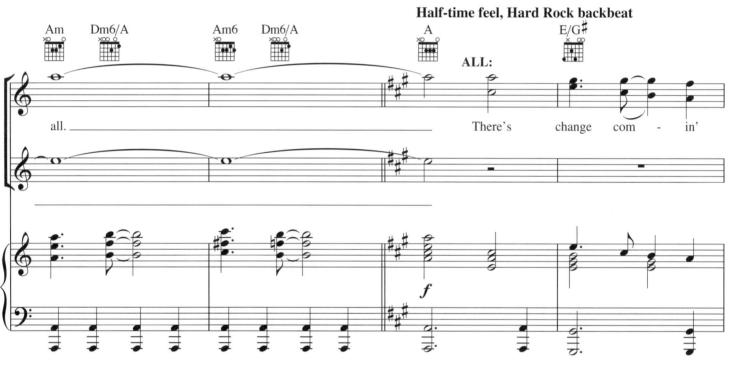